CHINA'S FIRST
EMPEROR AND HIS
TERRA–COTTA ARMY

CONTENTS

Waiting to be excavated

I、 THE QIN PEOPLE AND THE QIN STATE

According to legend Nu Xiu, the ancestorial mother of the Qin people, was a descendant of Zhuan Xun, who was also called Gaoyang. He was the grandson of the Yellow Emperor, one of the Five Great Emperors in Chinese history. Inscriptions on a stone bell excavated from No. 1 Tomb of a Qin Duke in Fengxiang County, Shaanxi Province said, " Gonghuan is an offspring and Gaoyang's soul is in heaven". This showed the Qin people considered themselves as offspring of Gaoyang. Nu Xiu became pregnant after she had eaten an egg of a swallow, and so the picture of a swallow became a symbol of the Qin tribe. Nu Xiu's son was Da Ye and Da Ye had a son called Da Fei.

8

◄ Color pottery kettle

▲ Golden ornament

Bronze incense burner with a phoenix
carrying a bronze ring in her mouth may
have some connection with the totem of
the Qin tribe. ▶

When Da Fei was head of the Qin tribe, he helped
King Shun raise birds and animals. Because of this good
work, King Shun gave him the surname of Ying. At the end
of Xia Dynasty (about 21st to 16th century B.C.), Fei
Chang, the great grandson of Da Fei left Xia Jie and went
to Shang (Shang Dynasty: about 16th to 11th century B.C.)
and fought with the Shang against the cruel Xia Jie. In the
middle of the Western Zhou Dynasty (about 11th century
to 771 B.C.) the Qin people lived in Tianshui, now Gansu
Province. Fei Zi, an ancestor of the Qin people was good
at raising horses and was asked by King Xiao of Zhou to
come into Huiwei (now Guizhen Town, Baoji, Shaanxi
Province) to raise horses for the imperial court. He did an
excellent job and was made a relative of the King who
bestowed him a territory Qin (east of Qingshui, now
Gansu Province) called Qin Ying. Since then people with
the surname Ying were call the Qin people and they had
their own conferred territory.

The Great Wall

▲ Excavating site of No.1 Tomb of a Qin Duke

The Qin people had the territory bestowed by King Ping of Zhou, but on this land there also lived the Shu and Di tribes. After fighting them for over 10 years, the Qin people gained control and settled. After 3 generations of dukes in over 80 years, a strong Qin state was built with its center in now Shaanxi Province, the western boundary in now Tianshui, Gansu Province and the eastern boundary in now Hua County, Shaanxi Province.

In 677 B.C. Duke Qin De moved the capital of the Qin State from a narrow valley at Pingyang (now Pingyang town, Baoji, Shaanxi Province) to the plain at Rongcheng (now Fengxiang County, Shaanxi Province). Rongcheng served as the capital of the Qin State for 294 years until 383 B.C. and about 20 generations of dukes lived there. During this period the Qin State, with rich land, became stronger and stronger, and Duke Qin Mu was one of 5 powerful dukes in the Spring and Autumn Time (770 to 476 B.C.). Many remains were discovered around Rongcheng and stone drums, bronze construction materials, tile ends, jade, gold were excavated. These discoveries and excavations showed there used to be many magnificent palaces in Rongcheng.

Duke Qin Xian succeeded to the throne in 384 B.C. and he was a great king. He revoked the rule of burying living slaves with their dead masters one year after his succession. To do battle with the Wei State, he moved his capital from Rongcheng to Leyang (now Lintong, Xi'an, Shaanxi Province), showing his determination to defeat the Wei. Also he moved to be away from the interference of the old power and to begin his reforms. After moving the capital, he issued the first field as a business decree, thereby allowing business activities in 378 B.C., speeding up the end of old productive relationships. He also carried out a system of five families as a unit to raise the position of slaves. He set up a county administrative system in 375 B.C.. The Qin's military force became strong and defeated the Wei army at Leyang (now Dali County, Shaanxi Province) and Shimen (now Yuncheng, Shanxi Province) in 366 B.C..

Qin bronze bell

▲ Panoramic view of Vault 1

Sculptures suggesting the First Emperor of Qin Unifying China ▶

Duke Qin Xiao succeeded the throne after the death of Qin Xian. He planned to follow the course set by his father and make the state stronger. He issued several decrees to attract talented people and Shang Yang came to the Qin State from the Wei State. As Prime Minister from 359 B.C. to 350 B.C. Shang Yang assisted Duke Qin Xiao to carry out a series of reforms, which were called Shang Yang's Reform in Chinese history. The reform sped up the change of economic structure, promoted development of society and formed a centralized political system. It created a solid foundation for the powerful Qin State and its unification of the whole country.

After several generations, the State of Qin successively conquered the states of Han, Zhao, Wei, Yan, Chu and Qi, all six strong states, ending the warfare and unifying China by 221 B.C.. A new page had been opened in Chinese history. Although the Qin Dynasty lasted only 15 years, it greatly influenced Chinese feudal society.

▲ Bronze standard weight

◀ Qin bronze bell

Picture of Ying Zheng,
the First Emperor of Qin

II. QIN SHIHUANG, THE FIRST EMPEROR IN CHINESE HISTORY

On a day in January, 259 B.C. a boy was born in Handan (now Handan City, Hebei Province) to the family of Yi Ren. Handan was the capital of the State of Zhao. Named Ying Zheng, the baby was to become the First Emperor of China.

The father Yi Ren was a grandson of King Qin Zhao and had 20 brothers. However, he wasn't the eldest son and his mother wasn't the favorite concubine of the Prince. In 279 B.C. King Qin Zhao wished to centralize his forces to attack the State of Chu, but he was afraid that he would be attacked from behind by the State of Zhao. So he met with King Zhao Hui in Mianchi and sent his grandson as a "hostage" to the State of Zhao. After the Qin had defeated the State of Chu, the Zhao and the Qin began to fight.

Yi Ren, still a hostage, was in danger, but a merchant and far-sighted politician, Lu Buwei, assisted him. Lu Buwei knew that King Qin Zhao was old and Crown Prince Xiao Wen would succeed him. Xiao Wen's favorite concubine Hua Yang would become Queen, but she didn't have a son and who would be the Crown Prince? Lu Buwei gave Yi Ren much gold for him to buy many unique gifts for Hua Yang to make her become fond of him. Yi Ren

▲ Money and coins used in the Warring States Time(475-221B.C.) ▲

Panoramic view of Vault I

▲ Remains of the Great Wall of Qin

changed his name into Zi Chu. Subsequently, Zi Chu was entitled the Crown Prince.

While Yi Ren was living in the State of Zhao, he married Zhao Ji with the help of Lu Buwei and they had a son named Ying Zheng (who was Qin Shihuang later). A legend had it that Qin Shihuang was really the son of Lu Buwei because Zhao Ji was pregnant when she married Yi Ren. So there are still arguments about the life story of Qin Shihuang.

Zi Chu (Yi Ren) eventually succeeded to the throne of the Qin Kingdom and was called King Zhuang Xiang. Lu Buwei was appointed Prime Minister. But King Zhuang Xiang died mysteriously after only 3 years. Crown Prince Ying Zheng, aged 13, succeeded him and appointed Lu Buwei Prime Minister and called him "God Father".

Zhao Ji became the mother of the King when she was young. Initially she had secret communications with Lu Buwei and later had a young man, Lao Ai, live with her at the Court with whom she had two sons. Because Ying Zheng was too young to administer the country two factions formed in the Court — one was the Officials Party led by Lu Buwei and the other was associated with the King's mother and led by Lao Ai. The two factions fought each other for control of the Court.

In 238 B.C., at the age of 22, Ying Zheng was coronated. Lao Ai tried to lead an army against the Qin King but the King attacked first and killed Lao Ai. The Qin King had his two stepbrothers killed and his mother Zhao Ji was placed under house arrest in a palace. Prime Minister Lu Buwei was dismissed and sent to (now) Henan Province. Two years later King Qin wrote to Lu Buwei, "What contribution did you make to the Qin Dynasty? Why were you conferred a large piece of land? Why were you called 'God Father'?" On receiving the letter, Lu Buwei knew he would be assassinated so he committed suicide. So the internal struggle for the throne ended, but Qin Shihuang's life story remained a secret.

After the coronation and victory with the struggle

▲ Inscriptions on stone in Yishan
Mountain (rubbing)

▲ Qin coins

for the throne, King Qin appointed Li Si Prime Minister and
made Wang Jian and his son generals. He carried out the
strategy of "making friends with distance states and fighting
against neighbouring states" and he conquered the six states
Han, Zhao, Wei, Chu, Yan and Qi successively from 230 B.C. to
221 B.C.. He established the first united centrally-ruled feudal
country. After the unification he named himself Qin Shihuang
(meaning the First Emperor of Qin) and established a feudal
bureaucratic system, promulgated county administrations,
standardized weights, money, Chinese characters and built the
Great Wall and "highways". The initiatives benefited the united
country and promoted development of the economy. But the
First Emperor did some autocratic acts such as burning books
and killing scholars, using a large conscripted labor force to
construct the Afang Palace and his mausoleum, levying heavy
rents and taxes and issuing cruel laws, which damaged
production and hindered progress in society. The first national
uprising of peasants in Chinese history occurred soon after his
death.

Qin Mausoleum

III. THE QIN MAUSOLEUM GARDEN

▲
An old photo of the Qin Mausoleum took in 1904

24

An old photo of the Qin Mausoleum took in 1904 ▼

Life and death were considered as two forms to imply value of a person. Qin Shihuang wished to live forever and searched for miraculous medicines to lengthen his life when he was alive. He disliked talking about death, but he knew that no one could break the laws of nature. He attempted to move his earthly empire to heaven and establish an underground empire that was as glorious as the one he ruled over when alive. This was the reason he built such a magnificent mausoleum.

Qin Shihuang began to build his mausoleum soon after he succeeded as King of the Qin State at age of 13. The construction of his mausoleum had not completed when he died at age of 51 in autumn 210 B.C.. Today the people who visit the Entombed Terra-cotta Army often wonder why Qin Shihuang chose Mount Li as his burial place, how many people took part in the construction, how large the Qin Mausoleum Garden was, and how the underground palace was.

WHY DID QIN SHIHUANG CHOOSE MOUNT LISHAN AS HIS BURIAL PLACE?

▲ A photo of the Qin Mausoleum took in 2004

Mount Lishan is an extinct volcano and there are many hot springs. The temperature of water flowing out of the ground reaches 43 degrees centigrade and the water contains minerals such as sodium carbonate, and has effects of curing skin diseases.

There were several reasons for Qin Shihuang to choose Mount Lishan as his burial place. From the point of view of a geomantic omen the place was ideal with mountains in the south and a river in the north. His back laid against the mountain and feet pointed to the river. Also the tombs of Qin Shihuang's ancestors were located in Zangyang, west of Lintong. As a descendant he should have his tomb east of Zangyang. It was then a rule that later generations were buried to the east of their older ones.

Qin Mausoleum

▲ Attendant vaults of the Qin Mausoleum are underground

HOW MANY PEOPLE TOOK PART
IN THE CONSTRUCTION?

According to the "Historical Records", about 700,000 people took part in the building of the Qin Mausoleum. Construction of the Mausoleum commenced soon after Qin Shihuang succeeded the throne. The number of builders may have varied over the construction period. Many extra workers were summoned after he conquered the other six states and became the First Emperor. Some may have been taken to work on the Afang Palace, and then were called back to the site of the Mausoleum when the First Emperor died in 210 B.C.. After sealing of the Mausoleum some may have been sent back to the Afang Palace again. So the total number of the builders could have been 800,000 at times.

HOW LARGE WAS THE QIN MAUSOLEUM GARDEN?

The archaeological workers have made a series of explorations in the Qin Mausoleum Garden, including the tumulus, the underground palace, and the ruins of the city walls. According to archaeological exploration the Qin Mausoleum Garden covered an area of 56.25 square kilometers and was enclosed by two city walls — the inner and outer walls. The inner wall measured 1,355 meters in length from north to south and 580 meters in width from east to west, with a circumference of 3,870 meters. A partition wall in the middle of the inner city divided them into two —the northern and southern parts. Further, a wall in the northern part divided it into two — the eastern and western zones.

▲　Eaves tile

FORMER GROUND CONSTRUCTION OF
THE QIN MAUSOLEUM GARDEN

CORNER TOWERS AT FOUR CORNERS
There was a tower at each corner of the inner
and outer city.

MAIN GATE TOWER
There were 6 gates at the inner
city and 4 at the outer city.

AUXILIARY BUILDINGS TO THE
RETIRING HALL.
A group of auxiliary buildings consisted of
ceremonial buildings, houses for officials,
dining houses and store houses.

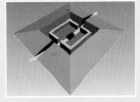

UNDERGROUND PALACE
35 meters beneath the surface of the ground, the underground palace was 170 meters long from east to west and 145 meters wide from north to south.

ENTRANCE TO THE RETIRING HALL
The Retiring hall was built as a palace implying Qin Shihuang still alive though he died.

PALACE
A group of structures was the retiring hall of Qin Shihuang and it was also the entrance to the underground palace.

▲ Painting of the sun, moon and stars in the shy unearthed from a tomb of the Western Han Dynasty (206 BC to 23 AD)

The outer city wall was 2,165 meters long from north to south, 940 meters wide from east to west with a circumference of 6,210 meters. There were gates in the inner city wall and the outer city wall facing in four directions. There were 6 gates in the inner city while there were 4 gates in the outer city wall. At each gate there was a structure called the gate building.

The tumulus, in the shape of a square pyramid, lies in the southern part of the inner city and it was about 170 meters high according to the record. After over 2,200 years of erosion by rain and wind and damage by man the tumulus is now 87 meters in height and its base is 350 meters in length from north to south and 345 meters in width from east to west. The top of the tumulus is a platform, which is 24 meters long from east to west and 10.4 meters wide from north to south, covering an area of 249.6 square meters. The tumulus was built of earth and rammed layer upon layer of earth can be seen now from the fault plane around it.

THE UNDERGROUND PALACE

The underground palace lies beneath the Qin Tumulus and was about 30 meters deep from the surface of the ground. The details of the underground construction are unknown but "The Historical Records" written by Sima Qian (145 to 90 B.C.) described it so: As soon as he became King of the Qin State, construction of his tomb was started at Lishan Mountain, and after he unified the country, over 700,000 conscripts from all parts of the country were summoned to work there. They dug through the subterranean streams and poured molten copper for the outer coffin. The tomb was filled with models of palaces, pavilions and offices, fine vessels, precious stones and rarities. Artisans were ordered to set up crossbows in the tomb so that any thief breaking in would be shot dead. There was a map of the sky on the ceiling and a topographical map on the floor with circulating mercury to represent the water of the earth. Eternal lamps were lit with man-fish grease (allegedly taken from a kind of four-legged and human-looking fish living in the East China Sea).

We are uncertain about the truth of the description, but a geophysical survey in the 1980s determined that there was in fact an area of 12,000 square meters of unnatural concentrations of mercury in the area under the tumulus.

33

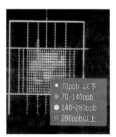

▲ Chart showing the changing of topsoil containing mercury around Qin Tumulus

▲ Chart showing an extremely high level of mercury in a large area of topsoil at the center of Qin Tumulus area

DIAGRAM OF THE UNDERGROUND PALACE OF QIN MAUSOLEUM

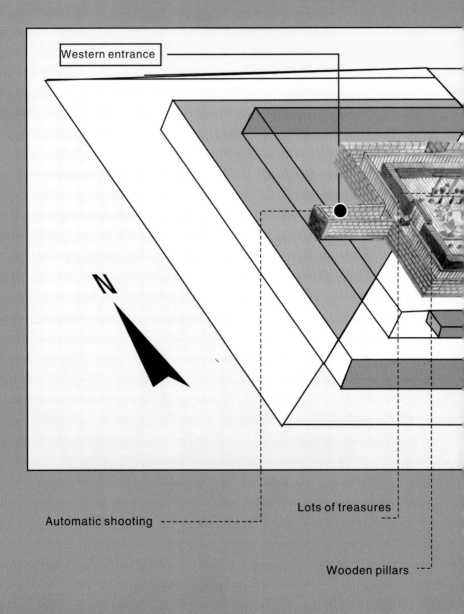

Western entrance

N

Automatic shooting

Lots of treasures

Wooden pillars

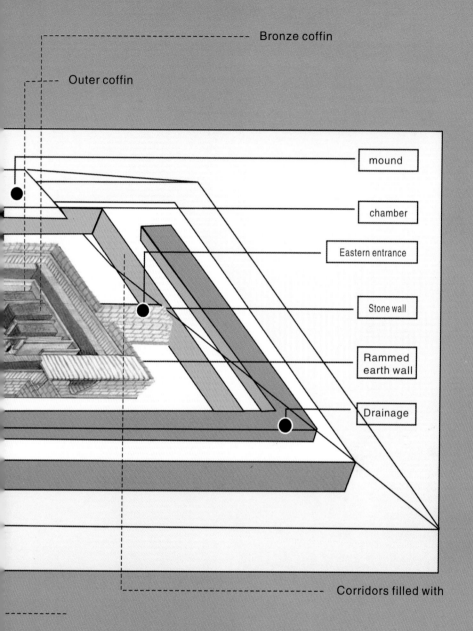

Bronze coffin

Outer coffin

mound

chamber

Eastern entrance

Stone wall

Rammed earth wall

Drainage

Corridors filled with

Vault of bronze water birds

IV. NEW DISCOVERIES IN THE QIN MAUSOLEUM GARDEN

The exploration and excavation around the Qin Mausoleum Garden has been preceded continuously and new discoveries have been made since the Terra-cotta Warriors and Horses were found in 1974. The main discoveries were the vaults of the stone armor and helmets, vaults of terra-cotta acrobatic figures, vaults of civil officials, vaults of rare birds and unfamiliar animals, pits of the bronze water birds and a bronze tripod, a bronze crane and lots of other cultural relics.

▼ Bronze ctane being unearthed

Terra-cotta musician

Terra-cotta acrobatic figure

Terra-cotta civil official

Bronze ctane

THE STONE ARMOR AND HELMETS

Farmers from Xiachen Village, southeast of the Qin Mausoleum were doing farm work when they found fired red soil in September, 1996. They reported it to the archaeologists who paid considerable attention because, from their experience, fired red soil usually implied a site of a ground construction or an underground construction. After exploratory drilling it was apparent it was an attendant vault. Researching on the site in April and May, 1997 they ascertained the shape and construction of the vault. From July 1998 to January 1999 the archaeologists again explored the vault and attempted to excavate sections.

The vault, located about 200 meters southeast of the Tumulus, has an oblong shape being 129 meters long from east to west and 105 meters wide from north to south, covering an area of 13,689 square meters. It is as large as Vault I of the Terra-cotta Warriors and Horses and is the largest attendant vault discovered so far between the inner and outer city walls. 145 square meters of the vault have been excavated now and many stone armor and helmets were unearthed.

◀ Stone ceremonia armorl

◄ Stone ceremonial helmet

The unearthed stone armor can be divided into three kinds: large, medium and small sized. Each suit of armor comprises more than 700 thin, overlapping stone tiles sewn together with copper thread. Each suit measures 80 centimeters long and weighs about 20 kilograms. The suits of armor are similar to those worn by the terra-cotta warriors. The overlappings were well made and have various shapes according to their position in the suit. Large overlapping tiles are 7 to 8 centimeters long and 3 to 4 centimeters wide and the small ones are 3 to 4 centimeters long and 1 centimeter wide, with both being 0.2 to 0.3 centimeters thick. At each end of the overlapping tiles there are 4 to 8 small holes for sewing.

The helmets are crowned with a flat circular stone from which jade and pearl ornaments hung. Overlapping stone shingles hang from small holes that line the circular stone's perimeter. The stone shingles hang 30 centimeters from the top of the helmet to the wearer's shoulders.

The suits of stone armor were placed in a regular order with four suits in each line forming four columns in each corridor similar to how the terra-cotta warriors stand in Vault I. It is thought that the armors originally were hung on wooden frames, but dropped to the ground after the wooden frames were burnt.

The stone armor couldn't be worn in battle because it was too heavy. The vault of armor, like the vaults of the Entombed Terra-cotta Army, was constructed because the First Emperor wanted everything after death to be like when he was alive.

THE BRONZE TRIPOD, THE FIRST
IN THE QIN MAUSOLEUM

The discovery of the stone armor vault provided an important clue for archaeologists to find other new attendant vaults. The archaeologists carried out systematic exploration around the vault of armors and in March 1999 found a new attendant vault 40 meters to the south. The vault is in " 凸 " shape and is 70 meters long from east to west and 12.5 to 16 meters wide from north to south, covering an area of 800 square meters.

A large bronze tripod vessle was unearthed from the vault standing 0.6 meters tall and weighing 212 kilograms. It is the largest Qin tripod ever found. The diameter of the tripod is 60.5 centimeters and the tripod is elaborately shaped with magnificent decorative patterns. The legs of the tripod feature animal face patterns. From the decoration and type the tripod is thought to have been made in the middle of the Warring States period (475 to 221 B.C.), or earlier, and to have served as a sacrificial vessel in a temple where the ancestors of the First Emperor of Qin were worshipped. Experts surmise that the tripod may have been moved from the temple to hide it during the turmoil at the end of the Qin Dynasty. The tripod is a valuable relic for the study of the ritual system and technique of bronze casting in the Qin Dynasty.

POTTERY FIGURES DEPICTING
A TROUPE OF ACROBATS

In the vaults between the inner and outer city walls of the Qin Mausoleum Cemetery Garden, archaeologists were surprised to find 11 life-sized pottery figures with distinctive characteristics scattered within an excavated area

Bronze tripod

of 9 square meters. Like those in the vaults of Terra-cotta Warriors and Horses, the pottery figures were broken into pieces, but each could be identified basically. The figures wore skirts just long enough to cover their hips. Diamond and star-shape patterns were painted on their skirts.

These figures are of different sizes and feature graceful poses. Three of them have been restored except for their severely damaged heads and were named No.1, 3 and 5 according to the order of discovery. The No.1 figure, comparatively small in size, stands straight with his hands clasped in front of his belly. No. 3 figure is the winner of a competition raising his right hand in the air with his waist swaying and his belly bulging. The No. 5 figure, about two meters tall after full restoration, stands upright grasping a horizontal tube-shaped bar with both hands, and holds a

Long vertical pole with his right arm. Originally all the figures were colorfully painted, but unfortunately the color has faded due to time or fire. The Chinese characters 咸阳亲 ” (Xianyang Qin) and “ 高 ” (Gao) were found inside figures No.1 and 5 and these are thought to be the names of the craftsmen and the name of places from where they came.

Experts believe that the pottery figures unear-thed from the vault depict acrobaticper formers bu-ried to entertain the First Emperor underground in his afterlife.

Terra-catta acrobatic figure

V. THE BRONZE CHARIOTS AND HORSES

The bronze chariots and horses were excavated just west of the Qin Tumulus. When an archaeological team drilled an exploratory hole 20 meter s west of the Qin Tumulus in July 1978, it discovered a round gold ornament from a depth of 7 metres, which was from a horse's head. After investigation, a large burial vault with 6 corridors and occupying a total area of 4,025 square meters was found. There were 6 rigs of painted wooden chariots and horses in the 3 southern corridors and 6 rigs of painted bronze chariots and horses in the northern ones.

With approval of the National Administration of Cultural Relics, the archaeological workers began to excavate the northern-most corridor in November 1980. The corridor was 11.8 meters long and 3.1 meters wide at the up part, but 7 meters long and 2.1 meters wide at the bottom. There was a large wooden coffin in the corridor and two rigs of painted bronze chariots and horses were in it. The two rigs were designated No.1 and No. 2. When excavated, the chariots and horses were severely damaged due to the decayed wooden coffin and the collapse of the earthen roofing. Fortunately their original locations were unaltered and pieces of the chariots and horses weren't missing.

The chariots and horses were moved to a restoration room of the Museum. After nearly 3 years of careful and painstaking restoration by archaeologists and other experts, No.1 chariot and horses was put on public display opening to the public on October 1, 1983. Four and a half years later, No.2 chariot and horses opened to the public on

◄　Location of the unearthed bronze chariots and horses

May 1, 1988. Now they are on display in a special exhibition hall.In ancient China each Emperor had his own special chariot and chariot team. When the First Emperor of Qin went on a tour of inspection, a very large chariot team followed. There were vanguard chariots, rear-guard chariots, company chariots of ministers and generals and company guard chariots in an order dictated by protocol. The unearthed bronze chariots imply the chariot system of the First Emperor.

The chariots and horses unearthed from the Qin Mausoleum Cemetery Garden were made of bronze and the decoration on them was of gold and silver. They are an exact half life-size model of the actual chariot, horse and driver. The bronze chariots, drawn by four horses with a single shaft, were placed one in front of the other. The front chariot, i.e. No.1 chariot, was named "High Chariot" and the charioteer stood on the chariot. The rear chariot, No.2, was named Security Chariot. No.1 chariot seems to protect the following No.2 chariot and the No.2 chariot appears to be for the Emperor's spirit to go on tours of inspection.

No.1 chariot and horses is 2.25 meters long and the total weight is 1,061 kilograms. The chariot has two wheels (diameter 66.4 centimeters), a single shaft and is drawn by four horses. The horses are almost the same, about 106 centimetres high, 109 centimetres long and each weights about 230 kilograms. The chariot body has an oblong shape and an umbrella stands in the middle. The canopy of the umbrella is a round bronze plate and the handle is shaped like bamboo. The charioteer stands under the umbrella, with a sword at his waist, holding 6 halters. There is a bronze bow in the front of the chariot and beside it is an arrow holder in which there are 54 arrows. On the other side there is a bronze shield which is the best preserved and earliest excavated.

The driver on No.2 Bronze
Chariot zhd Horses ▶

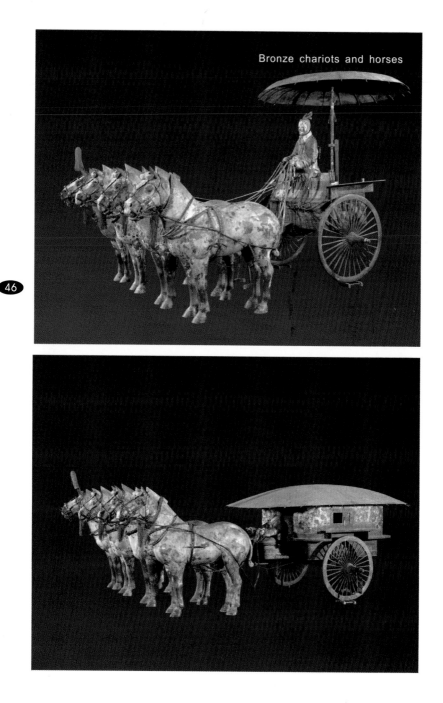

Bronze chariots and horses

The driver on No.1 Bronze Chariot and horses

The No.2 chariot and horses is 3.17 meters long and the total weight is 1,241 kilograms. The chariot had two wheels (diameter 59 centimeters) and a single shaft which is longer than that of No.1. The chariot is drawn by four horses which are the same as the horses of No.1 chariot. It has two rooms, the front one for the charioteer and the rear one perhaps for the spirit of the Emperor. The charioteer is kneeling in the front room with a sword at his waist, holding halters. The rear room has a door at the back and has a window in each of its two sides and in the front partition. The windows can be easily opened and closed and there are small holes in the windows for ventilation. When the windows are open, the inside of the chariot is cool. When they are closed, the inside is warm. So the chariot is also called the "air-conditioned chariot".

The chariots are composed of 3,462 pieces, of which 1,742 are made of bronze, 737 of gold and 983 are made of silver. Everyone who sees them can appreciate the advanced technology and admire the artistic shapes. For instance, the roof umbrella is only four millimeters thick while the window is one millimeter thick, with many ventilation holes. The horse tassels were made of bronze thread as thin as a hair. The horse necklets were welded together with 42 nodes of gold and 42 nodes of silver. Archaeologists can examine the welded joints only with the help of magnification. According to research, the making of the bronze chariot and horses involved different techniques such as casting, welding, riveting, mounting, embedding and carving. The chariots and horses showed the advanced design and construction of chariots and metallurgical techniques of the Qin Dynasty.

◄ Bronze chariots and horses
were under excavation

The driver on No.1 Bronze Chariot
and Horses ►

Patters on the bronze chariot

▲   The driver on No.1 Bronze
      Chariot and Horses

The bronze shield on No.1
Bronze Chariot and Horses   ▶

VI. THE TERRA-COTTA WARRIORS WERE DISCOVERED BY CHANCE

Qin Shihuang's terra-cotta warriors and horses were not recorded in the Chinese historical books. They disappeared when the Qin Dynasty was overthrown, but were discovered by an accident.

HOW WERE THE TERRA-COTTA WARRIORS DISCOVERED

When you visit Vault I of Qin's Terra-cotta Warriors and Horses, you will find in the south-eastern corner a sign saying "This is the well site of the discovery". The site of the well is 1,500 meters east of the Qin Shihuang's mausoleum and it used to be covered with brambles.

On March 29, 1974 some local farmers in Xiyang village, a small village 7.5 km. east of Lingtong County, Shaanxi Province were digging a well in the south of the village when they found a hole. They dug farther into the hole and found pottery fragments, bronze arrowheads and crossbows. The farmers at the site were astonished. They guessed there must be pottery statue of a god down there. In the evening some old men came to the site to burn joss sticks and pray to the god not to blame them.

When the local farmers did not know what to do with the "pottery God", Fang Shumin, a cadre responsible for the irrigation work from Yanzhai Township came to inspect the well. He knew something about archaeology. When he saw the pottery and brick fragments, he was sure they were cultural relics. He asked the local

52

The site of the well dug by local farmers ▼

❶ 这是发现
秦俑的井址
SITE OF THE WELL

farmers to stop digging the well and reported it to the Government of Lintong County. Zhao Kangmin and other two workers responsible for archaeological affairs from the Lingtong Culture Club were sent to assess the situation. The three were stunned by what they saw. They had never seen fragments of obviously large pottery figures. Unable to date them, they decided to take all the fragments back to the Culture Club. They told the farmers about the national policy of archaeology and asked them to hand in all the things they found. During the following two months Zhao Kangmin and his workers restored three figures. Because they were not sure of their historical period, they did not report the discovery to the relevant department.

By coincidence, Lin Anwen, a reporter from the Beijing-based China News Agency, was in Lingtong County to visit his family. He happened to see the three restored figures because his wife worked in the Culture Club. From experience he knew they were representations of Qin Shihuang's soldiers over 2,000 years old and rare treasures. After having interviewed Zhao Kangmin and made further investigations, he wrote a report entitled "The Terra-cotta Warriors and Horses of the Qin Dynasty Unearthed in the Tomb Area of the First Emperor". He sent the report to the Editor of "The People's Daily" and the report was published in the "Situation Collection" read by the circle of Chinese high officials. The news story caught the attention of the central government. On June 30 Li Xiannian, then China's Vice-premier, instructed, "I suggest that the State Cultural Relics Administration discuss with the Shaanxi Provincial Government what immediate action to take to properly protect this key relic site". Hence the terra-cotta figures became known to and cherished by the world.

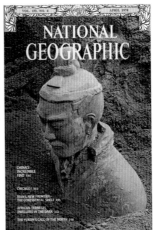

The cover page of April issue of "the National Geographic", a monthly magazine in the US in 1978 ▶

Location of the well dug by local farmers who found the Entombed Army in March 1974 ▼

Vladimir Putin President of Russia visiting the museum of the Entombed Army ▼

这是发现秦俑的井址。

Vaults of the Terra-corra Army under the exhibition hall and the old view of the former ground

Bill Clinton, the Former president of the US visiting the Museum of the Entombed Army

THE TERRA-COTTA FIGURES HAD
BEEN DISTURBED BEFORE

The vaults of terra-cotta warriors and horses were only about 5 meters deep beneath the surface of the ground but they were not recorded in Chinese history. They had been disturbed but not known to the public before they were discovered in 1974. When you visit the terra-cotta figures you may see pottery fragments under the ruin of timber crossbeams and traces of burning charcoal and ash on the partition walls. These illustrate the vaults were damaged. According to the recording and analysis of archeological excavation, it may have been Xiang Yu, the general who overthrew the Qin Dynasty together with another general, who destroyed the terra-cotta figures and other constructions within the tomb area at the end of the Qin Dynasty. He may have ordered his soldiers to dig up the vaults, damage the pottery figures and set fire to them. So the soldiers may have been the earliest people who found and destroyed the terra-cotta figures. From the excavations, we know that the ground above the vaults became wasteland late in the Western Han Dynasty (206 B.C — 24 A.D.). In one of the partition walls in Vault I a tomb of the early Western Han Dynasty was found and a coin made during the reign of the Han Emperor Wu was discovered in the tomb. Several tombs were found in Vault I and a husband and wife joint tomb of the Ming Dynasty (1368 —1644) was even lain beneath the brick floor of the terra- cotta figures. Two tombs of the Han Dynasty and 12 tombs of modern times were also found in Vault II. A well of 10 meters deep dug late in the Ming Dynasty or early in the Qin Dynasty (1644 —1911) was found in Vault II and there were many pottery fragments in it. From these we can see the terra-cotta figures were disturbed when these tombs were built and the well dug.

The local farmers said their ancestors had seen the pottery fragments but thought them " strange figures" when they built tombs or dug wells there. In August 1974 when the experts and archeological workers were making an experimental drilling in Vault I, He Wanchun, a 69-year-old local man told the experts a story. When he was 13

Terra-cotta being restored ▼

▲ Jacques Chirac, Mayor of Paris, France then visited the terra-cotta warriors in 1978

years old (about 1918), his father dug a well there. While digging he found a man-sized "strange figure" and he damaged an arm of the figure. The well had water then but became dry after two years. The farmers thought the "strange figure" may have drunk all the water so they took it from the well and beat it into pieces. He Wanchun showed the experts the place of the well where his father dug and it was in the site of Vault I. The terra-cotta figures were disturbed in history but they were not considered as treasures. Thanks to the local archeological workers and the reporter from the News Agency, they protected them and made them known to the public. Then with the help of governments at each level, the archeological experts have been excavating and studying them and have explained the real meaning of the terra-cotta warriors and horses.

Warriors waiting to stand up

Warriors waiting to stand up

VII. THREE VAULTS

The discovery of the terra-cotta figures attracted attention from all levels of the Chinese government and an archaeological excavation team was organized in 1974. The excavation of the mausoleum of the Qin First Emperor started and it has been going according to the plan since then.

IN VAULT I WAS THE MAIN FORCE OF THE TERRA-COTTA ARMY

Vault I was a rectangular shaped formation consisting of chariots and infantry and it was the main force of the Terra-cotta Army. In the long corridor at the eastern end of the vault stand 210 terra-cotta warriors in three rows. 204 face east and 3 at the northern and southern ends face north and south respectively. These three rows are regarded as the vanguard armed mainly with crossbows. In the long corridor at the western end of the vault also stand three rows of terra-cotta warriors. The outer western row faces west while the inner two rows face east. They are thought to be the rear guard. In the right and left corridors there are two rows of terra-cotta warriors each with the outside row facing outwards. Each row is about 184 meters long and around 180 terra-cotta warriors may be unearthed. In addition to the corridor around the circumference, there are 9 corridors in the vault and in each corridor there are four columns consisting of chariots and charioteers and infantrymen facing east. Thus there are 36 columns in the 9 corridors and each column is 178 meters long. There were over 6,000 terra-cotta warriors and about 45 chariots in Vault I. It is thought that the troops in Vault I are in a defensive formation, not marching or in an attacking formation because the warriors in outer lines had crossbows as their main weapons, which were used for long distant archery, not short range attack; while there is a row around the circumference facing outwards

Plan of the vaults of Qin's Terra-cotta Army ▼

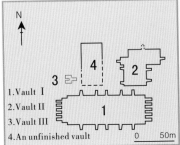

N ↑

1. Vault I
2. Vault II
3. Vault III
4. An unfinished vault

0   50m

N

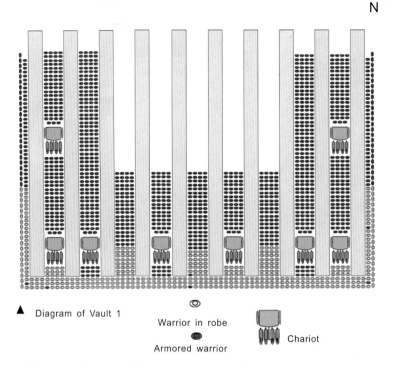

▲ Diagram of Vault 1

Warrior in robe

Armored warrior

Chariot

so the army does not have a concentrated attacking direction; and most of the vanguard at the eastern end are in robes and not armored.

VAULT II CONTAINED MULTI-PURPOSE BATTLE FORMATIONS

When the archaeological workers were doing an exploratory drilling around Vault I, they discovered the second vault to the north of the eastern end of Vault I on April 23, 1976 and called it Vault II. From May 1976 to August 1977 an archaeological team did a proving excavation on Vault II and analyzed that the pit in an "L" shape covered an area of 6,000 square meters, half the size of Vault I. It consists of two parts or four arrays with the northern part in a rectangular shape and the southern part in a square shape. In the proving excavation there were

Part view of Vault I

63

unearthed 11 wooden chariots, 67 pottery chariot horses, 32 terra-cotta cavalrymen, 29 pottery horses, 163 terra-cotta warriors and about 900 various bronze weapons.

Vault II is divided into four arrays according to its shape and the different military forces. The first array, the eastern protruding part of the pit is 26.6 meters long and 38.8 meters wide. There are 174 standing archers along the four sides and 160 kneeling archers in 8 columns in the middle. The formation consisting of standing archers and kneeling archers allowed archers to shoot in turns. The second array, located in the south of the vault, is 52 meters long and 48 meters wide including 8 passage ways. It is composed of 64 chariots, 8 in each row and 8 in each column, and each chariot carries three warriors. The middle one is a charioteer. The third array in an oblong shape is located in the middle of the vault, 68 meters long and 16 meters wide. It is a formation of chariots, infantrymen and cavalrymen. There are 8 columns and in each column there are 6 chariots. Behind the chariots there are infantrymen and a few cavalrymen. The fourth array, located in the north of the vault, is 50 meters long and 20 meter wide. It is composed of 6 chariots and 124 saddled horses and cavalrymen. The four arrays make up a large formation but they also could operate as four independent arrays.

VAULT III WAS THE COMMAND HEADQUARTERS

Vault III was discovered to the northwest of the Vault I and to the west of Vault II by archaeologists in an exploratory drilling on May 11, 1976. The excavation started in 1989 and it was found to be much different from Vault I and II. It opened to the public in September 1989.

Vault III is in a "U" shape with a total area of 500 square meters. There is a sloping entrance to its east opposite which is a chariot and horse stable. On both sides of the stable there is a side room. From the pit there was unearthed 1 wooden chariot, 68 terra-cotta warriors, 4 terra-cotta horses and 34 bronze weapons. The excavated figures and horses were severely damaged and most of the heads and some other body parts could not be found. It is a

AND HIS TERRA-COTTA ARMY

mystery who damaged them and when they did it.

The arrangement of the pottery figures is quite different from that in Vaults I and II in which the warriors are in battle formation. By contrast, those in Vault III are arrayed facing each other along the walls in rows. The figures are much fewer than those in Vaults I and II, and they appear to be guards of honor. The tie styles and weapons of the 68 warriors are also different from those in the other two pits where the weapons were long-range crossbows and arrows and short weapons such as spears, barbed spears and swords. In Vault III there was discovered only one kind of weapon called a *shu* which hadn't any blades and is believed to have been used by guards of honor.

The chariot in Vault III is different from that in Vaults I and II and the former was decorated with bright colors and had a 42-centimeter diameter painted canopy. There were 4 warriors in the chariot, but no weapons. From the dress and hand gestures of the warriors it seems that their position is higher than the charioteers but lower than the officers in the other two vaults. So the chariot is believed to be a command chariot and Vault III is most likely the headquarters directing the underground army.

65

▼ Former view of the ground where the Terra-cotta Army excavated before

Panoramic view of Vault I

Vault II exhibites while being excavated

Vault III-the headquarters of the Terra-cotta Army

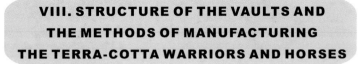

VIII. STRUCTURE OF THE VAULTS AND THE METHODS OF MANUFACTURING THE TERRA-COTTA WARRIORS AND HORSES

The vaults of the terra-cotta warriors and horses were created over 2,200 years ago, then damaged by fire, but the magnificent appearance of their large structure can still be seen. More secrets will be discovered by archaeological excavation and study of the structure of the vaults, the types of terra-cotta warriors, the battle formation of the terra-cotta army and the methods of making the terra-cotta figures and horses.

68

◄ Kneeling archer

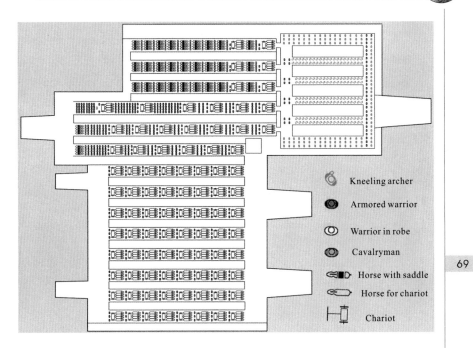

Kneeling archer

Armored warrior

Warrior in robe

Cavalryman

Horse with saddle

Horse for chariot

Chariot

▲ Diagram of Vault II

▼ Remains of the wood roof

Part View of Vault I

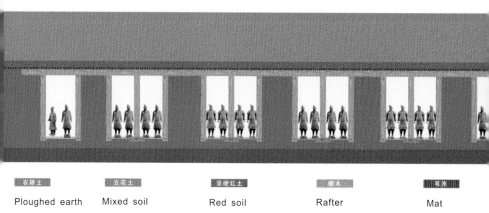

农耕土	五花土	坚硬红土	棚木	幕席
Ploughed earth	Mixed soil	Red soil	Rafter	Mat

Diagram of the vault structure

| 柱头枋木 | 夯土隔墙 | 铺地砖 | 生土 | 0 1 2m ^米 |
| Pole | Partition Wall | Paved brick | Soil | |

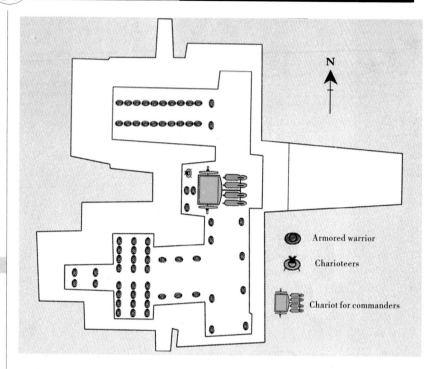

N

Armored warrior

Charioteers

Chariot for commanders

▲ Diagram of Vault III

Vault III—the headquarters
of the Terra-cotta Army ▶

ARCHITECTURAL STRUCTURE OF THE VAULTS

The three attendant vaults, covering a total area of 40,000 square meters, had their special architectural forms and characteristics. They were a total battle array, but could also be divided into independent army units.

Vault I, in a rectangular shape, is 230 meters long, 62 meters wide, covering an area of 14,260 square meters. It is 1,225 meters away from the Qin tumulus, in a straight line from the northeastern corner of the outer City Wall of the Qin Mausoleum. In the vault there are 10 two-meter high earth-rammed walls, which divided the vault into 9 corridors from north to south and an outside circumferential corridor. There are 5 sloping entry ramps in each four sides of the vault.

The shape of the Vault II is different from that of the Vault I. It is in the shape of a carpenter's square, covering about 6,000 square meters. There are two sections: the northern part is square-shaped and the southern part is rectangular-shaped. Both are an earth-wood structure in the form of roofed corridors. The longest part from east to west is 120 meters and the widest part from north to south is 98 meters. There are two sloping entrances in the eastern, western and northern ends respectively.

Vault III, called "the headquarters pit" is in shape of a "U", covering an area of 520 square meters. In its eastern end there is a sloping entry ramp, 11.2 meters long, 3.7 meters wide, opposite which is a chariot and horse stable. On both sides of the stable there is a side room.

As the underground structures are on a large scale and with special forms, careful plans should be made for each process according to the design. The plans of the three vaults are different, but the three dimensional method of construction is the same. They are all earth-wood structures in the form of roofed corridors. The process of construction is as follows.

Armored lower-ranking official ▶

Cavalryman

Cavalryman

Long pits were dug first, and then soil was piled up and rammed to create a base and the partition walls. When the partition walls were built, wood panels were placed against the walls. Across these vertical panels, rafters were placed and then covered with mat, a 10 to 30 centimeters thick layer of fine soil and finally a 2-meter thick covering of earth. The floor was paved with brick. After the corridors had been built, the chariots and terra-cotta warriors and horses were carried into them through the sloping entrances and arranged in order. After completing the arrangement, the entrances were shut off with wood lining and the sloping ramps were filled with rammed earth. It finally formed a completely sealed underground structure.

HOW MANY TYPES OF WARRIORS AND HORSES ARE THERE?

The terra-cotta warriors unearthed from the three vaults can be divided into three types: infantry, charioteers and passengers, and cavalry. The infantry, including figures in lines of battle formation and figures in front and behind the chariots, can be subdivided into generals, officers and soldiers. The generals and officers are of two types: those wearing robes (light armored figures) and others wearing armor (heavy armored figures). The soldiers can also be subdivided into figures holding cross bows, those holding short-handled weapons and others holding long-handled weapons. The figures holding cross bows are standing archers and kneeling archers. The figures holding short-handled weapons have swords or hooks. The figures holding long-handled weapons

◄ Armored lower-ranking official

have spears, halberds, lances, "shu" (a weapon without a blade used by guards of honor) or others weapons. On each ordinary chariot, there were two soldiers, and a charioteer. On the commander's chariot there is a general, a charioteer and one or two soldiers. The cavalry is divided into those in the battle formation and those in the rear.

The pottery horses are of two types: those drawing chariots and those for riding.

▼ Kneeling archer

Cavalryman

Heavy-armored archer

HOW WERE THE FIGURES AND HORSES MADE?

The terra-cotta figures and horses were all broken when unearthed. From the broken pieces it can be analyzed that there were 4 steps in manufacture: molding and sculpting, carving, firing and painting.

The bodies of the terra-cotta warriors were made in molds, or by sculpting. The feet, hands and legs were made by hand and then joined to the body. The most sophisticated technique was THE manufacture of the head. Two molds were used to make the face and other parts of the head and then the two halves were joined together. ears, nose, hair and moustache were made separately and added later. In order to stop the figures toppling over, a plinth was added beneath the feet of the warrior. The roughly made models were carved exquisitely in detail according to their personal characters and rank. After the figures had been made they were carried into kilns and fired. In order to prevent the figures from deforming or exploding, one, two or three small holes were made in the body before firing. The last step of manufacture was painting with color.

80

The technique of making the terra-cotta horses was similar to that of the terra-cotta warriors. The head, body, legs, and tail of the horse were made in molds separately. The ears were made by hand. They were then all joined together and the joins covered with clay. Like the terra-cotta warriors, they were carved, fired and painted with color.

◄ Pottery sculptures showing how the terra-cotta warriors were made

◄ Pottery sculptures showing how the terra-cotta horses were made

Charioteers

Warrior

ARTISTIC VALUE OF THE TERRA-COTTA ARMY

The approximately 8000 life-sized Terra-cotta Warriors and Horses were unique in the history of sculpture in the world. With characteristics of realism, a simple style, but fine technique and the grand appearance of the battle formations, they represent the art of the ancient Orient which can compare with the art of Greece and Rome.

The terra-cotta figures are both realistic and representative in style. Individually, all the terra-cotta figures are alike, motionless and standing upright, but their makers individualized them through different facial expressions and face modeling. The faces of warriors are square jawed with narrow foreheads suggesting power and strength, while most faces of the vanguard have a square forehead and a narrow jaw indicating intelligence. Different configurations of facial features are combined

◄ Terra-cotta warrior

▲   Terra-cotta warriors

with different face types to create varied facial expressions. So the warriors were made lively and vividly and their nationality, positions and ranks can be told from their features, uniforms, weapons and postures. The terra-cotta horses were made alike exactly and their direct relations were very clear. Many kinds of traditional skills such as modeling, sculpturing, carving, relief and painting were used in the making of the Terra-cotta Warriors and Horses, which showed the talent of the Qin people.

The unearthed terra-cotta figures and horses you see in the pits now are greenish gray, but this is not their original color. The surviving colors on the figures and horses when they were first unearthed included red, white, green, purple and orange-yellow on the robes, black on the armor and pink on the faces, hands and feet.

The art of the sculpture created a new field, demonstrating the great achievementS of large-scale sculpture in ancient China. It was a successful example in Chinese history of sculpture art.

Pottery sculptures showing how the terra-cotta figures were painted

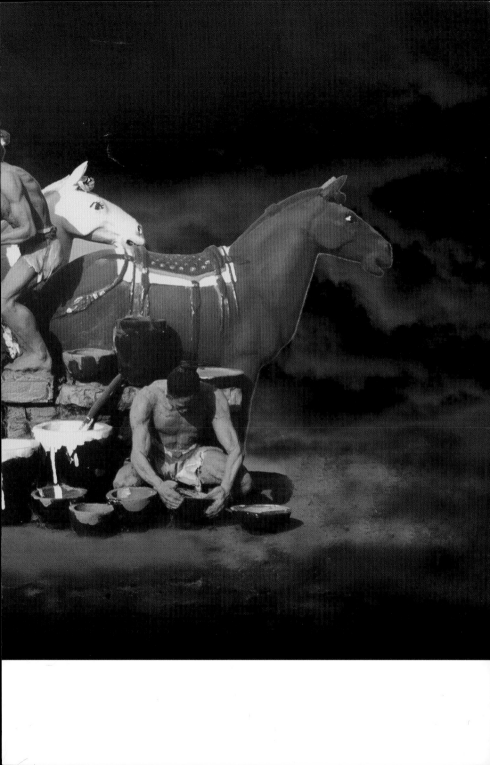

IX. WEAPONS UNEARTHED
FROM THE VAULTS

The weapons unearthed from the vaults were mainly made of bronze and a few were made of iron. They are bronze swords, hooks, halberds, lances, spears, crossbows and arrowheads, totaling in all 40,000 pieces. They can be divided into four categories: long-range weapons (crossbows), long-shafted weapons, short weapons and weapons for guards of honor. In the battle formation most warriors held crossbows and some had spears. The combination of long-range weapons and short-range weapons can be of mutual assistance and protection.

Both the bow and the crossbow are for shooting arrows but they are different. The bow is stretched and shot by muscle power while the crossbow is stretched and shot by mechanical action. The crossbows unearthed from the vaults of the Entombed Terra-cotta Army consist of three parts: the bow, the handle and the trigger. The bow had been 1.3 to 1.4 meters long, but had rotted away and only the trigger, which was made of bronze, remained. From the remains we can judge there were at least three kinds of crossbows in the Qin Dynasty.

The long-shafted weapons held by the terra-cotta warriors are dagger-axes, spears and halberds while the short weapons are swords mainly. .

The *Yue* and the *Shu* were weapons used by guards of honor. The *Yue* came from the battle-axe but it had lost its combat function and was used as a symbol of a special status in the Qin Dynasty. The *Shu* was a weapon of honor without blades and it was cast and then polished. About 30 pieces of the Shu were excavated from Vault III and they showed that the *Shu* was used as a weapon of honor, but not a real weapon in battles in the Qin Dynasty.

The chemical analysis of the weapons unearthed from the vaults of the Entombed Terra-cotta Army reveal that the weapons contain

▼ Bronze spear

copper (Cu), tin (Sn) and lead (Pb) mainly and also iron (Fe), manganese (Mn), magnesium (Mg), cobalt (Co), Zinc (Zn), titanium (Ti), chromium (Cr) and molybdenum (Mo). The content of tin compared to copper gave the bronze a different hardness. The higher content of tin, the harder the bronze will be. The percentage of tin in the swords unearthed from the vaults is 18 to 20 per cent by measurement.

The unearthed weapons revealed the secrets of metallurgical technology of the Qin Dynasty. The weapons were cast, ground and polished. To prevent rusting, the swords and the arrowheads were coated with a thin layer (10 micron) of oxidized chromium, which shows that they were oxidized with chromium during manufacture. The technology of chromium coating was invented by a German in 1937 and by an American who registered a patent in 1950, but in China the chromium-coating technique was employed in the making of weapons over 2,200 year ago. It is truly a wonder in the metallurgical history of the world. The weapons coated with chromium were still bright and sharp without rust when unearthed although they had been in the ground for over 2,200 years.

It was also discovered that hundreds of crossbows triggers could be used interchangeably because their bolts and suspending knives were manufactured to a tolerance of 1 millimeter. The arrowheads are divided into four kinds. The edges of the three sides of the arrowheads of the same kind had a tolerance of 0.15 millimeter. From this, it can be seen that weapon manufacture was already standardized to meet the needs of war. This also shows that the Chinese metallurgical technology had reached a high standard and ranked the first in the world during the Qin Dynasty.

Triggers on the
crossbows ▶

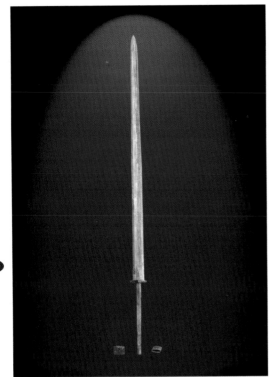

Bronze sword

Bronze halberd

Bronze *Pi*

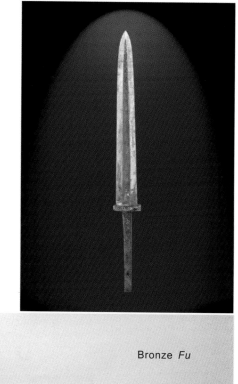

Bronze *Fu*

◀ Bronze hook

Bronze spear ▶

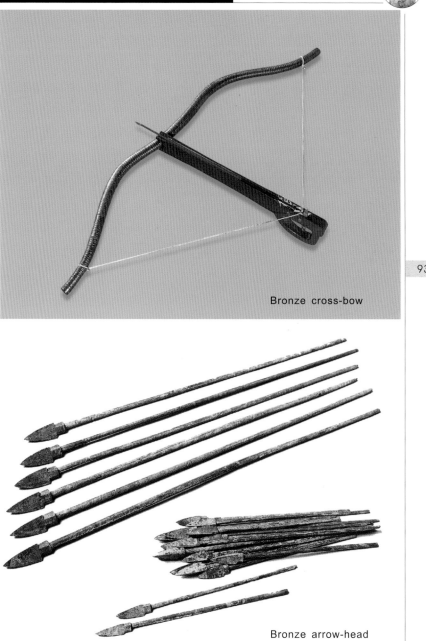

Bronze cross-bow

Bronze arrow-head

Terra-cotta warrior

Terra-cotta warrior

95

X. THE TERRA-COTTA ARMY REPRESENTED THE REAL MILITARY FORCE OF THE QIN DYNASTY

The location of the entombed terra-cotta army is 1,500 meters from the Qin tumulus and 1,225 meters from the outer wall of the Qin Mausoleum Garden. Like the real army, it remained outside of the city, but defended the city. There will be about 6,000 terra-cotta warriors unearthed from the three vaults according to the estimate of archaeologists and they can be divided into three types: infantry, charioteers and passengers, and cavalry.

The infantry included generals, officers and warriors and the warriors can be subdivided into figures holding cross bows, those holding short-handled weapons and others holding long-handled weapons. The figures holding cross bows are standing archers and kneeling archers.

There were two soldiers and the charioteer on each ordinary chariot while there was a general, the charioteer and one or two soldiers on the commander's chariot.

The discovery of the terra-cotta warriors and horses helps us know more about the uniforms of the army in the Qin Dynasty. They wore a hat, robe, trousers, belt and shoes. The hat worn by warriors was a crown-hat, or a cap. The crown-hat, which was a symbol of rank, was usually worn by generals. The crown-hat with a single sloping flat plate was for lower officers. The crown-hat with double flat plates was for middle level officers and generals. The crown-hat with special double

Terra-catta warrior
▼

ties was for high generals. Caps were of two different types, one for armored warriors and the other for the cavalry.

Most terra-cotta warriors wore long robes long enough to cover the knees. The robes were of two types: double layered robes for high generals and single layer robes for other generals and warriors. A short-sleeved robe was found which was for the cavalry. This was adapted from robes worn by people of the Hu nation who were skilled horse riders. It was also found that warriors wore a round collared shirt under their robes. Trousers worn by warriors had both long and short legs. The long legged trousers reached the ankles and were tied at the ankle. These were worn mainly by generals, officers and the cavalry. The short legged trousers didn't cover the knees. Most of the armored warriors and charioteers had long bindings wound around their calves for protection of the calves.

Warriors wore shoes made of gunny cloth. The shape of the shoe was like a ship with a lower front and a high rear. It had a thin sole. The color remains show that the shoes were painted black or brown but the edges were red. The cavalry wore 15 cm high boots. From the color remains it is thought the boots were painted red, or green.

The clothes and shoes worn by warriors show a combination of the styles of the Han people and the Hu people (a minority nationality in China). The main colors of the clothes were green, red, blue and purple with strong contrasts. The study of the various colors and styles of the clothing show that the uniforms were not provided by the army, but were made by the soldiers themselves.

Part of the terra-catta warrior ▶

97

Parts of the terra-corra warrior

Parts of the terra-corra warrior

XI. RESTORATION AND PROTECTION OF THE TERRA-COTTA WARRIORS AND HORSES

The Qin mausoleum and its attendant vaults including the vaults of terra-cotta warriors and horses are treasures of China and were listed as the world's cultural heritage. They are under national protection.

The entombed warriors were severely damaged by fire and by being buried for over 2,200 years. There was hardly a complete warrior or horse when excavated. They were broken into pieces. How are they restored? When a terra-cotta figure is discovered, the archaeological workers make records of the location, its situation and the relationship between the figure and others around it. At the same time they take photos and mark numbers on the figures. Before restoration, the workers analyze the figure and become familiar with the structure and its attachments. Then a plan about the process and methods of restoration is made. The restoration is a careful scientific work. The following is a rough, but basic of the restoration.

Firstly, the archaeological workers classify the unearthed fragments of a warrior according to their shapes, patterns and colors, and then try to match the fragments and make marks on them.

Secondly, with a small knife or a brush, the workers remove earth from the fragments, especially from the edges, and clean them with water. Then the fragments are left to dry.

Thirdly, the workers clean the edges of the fragments with a special liquid, and apply epoxy resin to glue the fragments together from the bottom up. While gluing, the figure is assembled in several parts to allow the glue to solidify without breaking. A reinforcing bar is put inside the legs to strengthen them. Pieces of cloth saturated with glue are stuck over the joints to give them strength.

Fourthly, after the fragments are dry, the workers cover the cracks on the figure.

▼
Terra-cotta figures being restored

Fifthly, the figure is made to look as old as they are.

The protection of the colors on the terra-cotta warriors and horses is a major task in the protection of the terra-cotta figures. After many years of hard work by archaeologists, achievements have been made.

The composition of the colors has been analyzed and it is found that the main composition of the colors in the first layer is Chinese raw lacquer. The main reason for the damage of the colors is that the Chinese raw lacquer curls up when the terra-cotta figure dries out. That caused the colors to drop off the terra-cotta figures. The archaeologists have now found an effective method of protection. When a protective liquid is sprayed onto the painted terra-cotta figures several times, the colors will not break off. This method is now used in the excavation site of Vault II. The excavation and successful protection of kneeling archers are of importance. They will reveal the original colors of the terra-cotta warriors and horses, and provide the experts with valuable data for the study of painting technology, color of clothes and composition of colors in the Qin Dynasty.

When the experts studied composition of the colors, they found a chemical mixture named "copper barium silicate" in the color purple. It is a great surprise that this chemical mixture is a side product of studying synthesized super-conductive material in 1980s. It has not been found in nature. This finding shows that Chinese people had mastered a technique to make a mixture of material with a synthesizing technique 2,200 years ago. It must be another wonder in the history of science and technology of the world.

Warriors being excavated ▼

Green-faced head of a warrior

Kneeling archers with original colors

▲ Terra-cotta warriors being restored

▼ Warriors waiting
to stand up

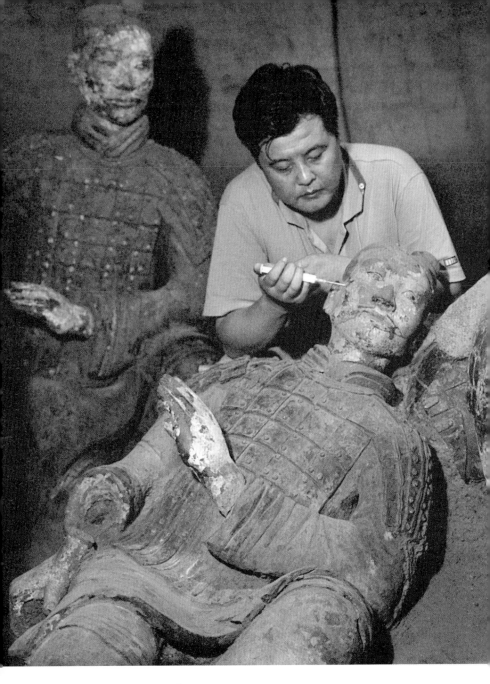

Warriors under protection

XII. LATEST DISCOVERIES IN THE VAULTS OF THE TERRA-COTTA ARMY

The excavation in the vaults of the Terra-cotta Army has been going on since 1974 and many new discoveries have appeared steadily. When the archaeological workers excavated in Vault II, they cleaned earth off the collapsed rafters at the first stage. From 1999 they began the second stage to excavate the Terra-cotta Warriors and Horses beneath the rafters. Six kneeling painted terra-cotta

◀ Kneeling archers with original colors

archers in an aiming stance and a green-faced archer were discovered. The colors on the archers were well preserved. Now some archers have been excavated and some are half unearthed. It is unique to discover warriors with well preserved colors. For various reasons, the color dropped off the terra-cotta warriors and horses when they were unearthed. The new discovery is exciting news. In order to let visitors watch the new discovered kneeling archers clearly, 4 telescopes have been set up on the side of Vault II.

The composition of the color on painted parts varies. Some archers had gelatin applied first and then one or two thick layers of pigments were applied. Other archers had gelatin painted on some parts without any covering color. The archers were painted with various colors. The faces are pink and the necks are pinkish green. The hands are pinkish white, or red, and the robes are green. The legs are pinkish green, or red, and the hair is black. The eyes were first painted white and then black was used to mark out the pupils. The brightly colored archers are masterpieces for they convey a vigorous feeling.

A warrior with a green face (excepting its black hair, beard and eyes) was found on September 10, 1999. It is the only discovery of this kind since excavation began. Unlike the other warriors with pinkish-red or pinkish-white faces, this is a green- faced warrior. Some said this is the result of a chemical reaction of the color with materials buried beneath the ground for a long time. Others said it was painted by a craftsman imitating the dark-skinned people. But some said it was made by a craftsman who practiced a joke. Which saying is right? It needs a further study.

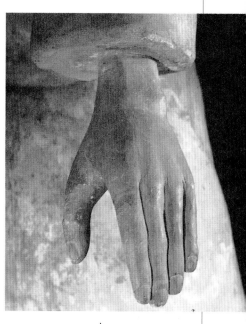

▲
Kneeling archers
with original colors

临马公路

北 Highway

入口 Entrance

市場 Market

陈列厅 秦俑出土文物展厅 Exhibition Hall of Unearthed Cultural Relics of Qin Dynasty

WC

票处 Ticket selling windows

口 trance

WC

特别推荐书目：
《秦陵秦俑百谜》
《秦陵·秦俑最新发现》（中英
日韩德法意西）（16K本大图录）
《凝视秦陵秦俑》（中英日韩）
（32K本中图录）
《秦都秦陵秦俑传说故事》
《秦陵秦俑最新图录》
（中英日韩）（64K本小图录）
《寻宝图—西安、秦俑博物馆、
华清池自助游》（手绘图）
《风流华清池》（中英日韩）
（64K本小图录）
《西安，为您收藏3000年》
（64K本小图录）
《秦始皇皇陵兵马俑》（中英
文明信片16张）
新丝路图文工作室
常年免邮费为您服务。
（E-mail:zt1965376@sina.com
TEL:13772199652）。
陕西旅游出版社新丝路图文工作室
不断出版有关陕西文化精品图书。

图书在版编目（CIP）数据

中国第一位皇帝及他的兵马俑军队=China's First Emperor and His
Terra-Cotta Army/李强，石磊编著。
西安：陕西旅游出版社，2005.5(2006.11重印)
(新丝路丛书/齐秀主编)
ISBN7-5418-2185-3

Ⅰ中… Ⅱ.①李…②石… Ⅲ.秦始皇陵—兵马
俑—简介—英文 Ⅳ.k878.9

中国版本图书馆CIP数据核字（2006）第134706号

CHINA'S FIRST EMPEROR
AHD HIS TERRA-COTTA ARMY

Executive Editor：zang yun

Chinese Written by Li Qiang Shi Lei

English Translated by Liu Daoxuan and Liu Qian

English Proof-read by Robert Dorning (Australia)

Photographs by Xia Juxian and Guo Yan

（本书中乐人俑、青铜雁摘自《秦始皇陵及兵马俑》一书，请摄影者与总编部联系）

陕西旅游出版社出版发行

（西安长安北路56号 邮政编码710061）

新华书店经销 商南顺意印务有限公司印刷

889×1194mm 32开本 3.5印张 50千字

2006年11月第1版 2006年12月第2次印刷

ISBN 7—5418—2185—3/K · 206

004000